W9-BWF-419

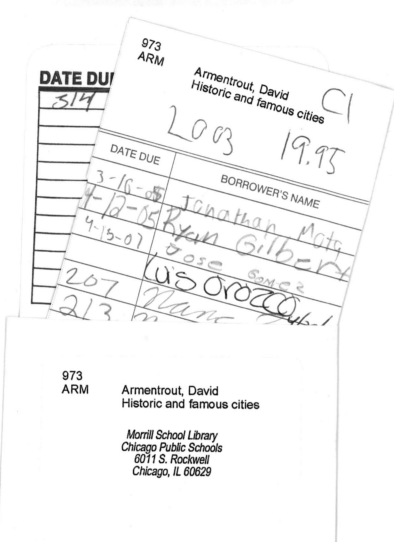

973
ARM

Armentrout, David
Historic and famous cities $C1$

ℒℴℴℬ   19.95

DATE DUE	BORROWER'S NAME
3-16-05	Jonathan Mata
4-12-05	Ryan Gilbert
4-13-07	Jose Gomez
207	Luis Orozco
213	Nanc

DATE DU

314	

The Rourke Guide
to State Symbols

HISTORIC AND FAMOUS CITIES

David and Patricia Armentrout

The Rourke Publishing LLC
Vero Beach, Florida 32964

www.rourkepublishing.com

PHOTO CREDITS:
©James P. Rowan pages 5, 11, 17 top, 24 bottom, 38, 39
©Alfred A. Michaud page 28 bottom
©National Park Service page 7
©Corel page 48
©Helena Area Chamber of Commerce page 26
©North Dakota Tourism Department page 32 bottom
©State of West Virginia page 46
©Old Cowtown Museum, Historic Wichita-Sedgwick County, Inc., Wichita, Kansas page 18
©Corbis pages 6, 8, 13, 14, 16, 23, 25, 31, 33, 40, 42, 47
©PhotoDisc pages 6 top, 9, 10, 12, 15, 17 bottom, 19, 20, 21, 22, 24 top, 27, 28 top, 29, 30, 32 top, 34, 35, 36, 37, 41, 43, 44, 45

COVER ILLUSTRATION: Jim Spence

EDITORIAL SERVICES:
Pamela Schroeder

Library of Congress Cataloging-in-Publication Data

Armentrout, David and Patricia
    Historic and famous cities / David and Patricia Armentrout
        p. cm. — (The Rourke guide to state symbols)
    Includes index
    Summary: Describes a variety of historic and famous cities in the United States, from Mobile, Alabama to Jackson, Wyoming.
    ISBN 1-58952-084-X
    1. United States—History, Local—Juvenile literature. 2. Cities and towns—United States—Juvenile literature. [1. Cities and towns. 2. United States—History, Local.] I. Armentrout, Patricia, 1960- II. Title. III. Series

E180 .A76 2001
973—dc21   2001031978

Printed in the USA

TABLE OF CONTENTS

INTRODUCTION

There are thousands of historic and famous cities in the United States. What makes a city famous? There are many reasons a city becomes famous. Natural attractions like oceans, parks, or scenic mountains help nearby cities grow popular. People love to go places where they can enjoy nature. Miami and Honolulu, for instance, are popular and famous for their beautiful beaches.

People also visit cities if there is something special or interesting about them. New York and San Francisco are often visited because they have many fine restaurants and fancy hotels. These cities are famous and historic. San Francisco's history includes its population boom in 1849—the beginning of the California gold rush. New York City's history dates back to the 1500s with its first explorers. It's now the largest city in the United States.

Take a tour of some of the most interesting cities in the United States. Read about the reasons people choose to visit these famous and historic cities.

ALABAMA

Mobile

Mobile is one of the largest cities in Alabama. It was settled by the French in the early 1700s. Today Mobile is known for its beautiful gardens and old houses that show off their French designs. Tourists visit the Oakleigh Mansion and the Exploreum Science Museum.

Mobile is located at the mouth of the Mobile River. On the city's waterfront is a favorite attraction—the World War II *USS Alabama* battleship.

ALASKA

Anchorage

Anchorage was founded in 1914. Anchorage grew in industry and in population because of the discovery of oil nearby. Anchorage is now Alaska's largest city.

People are drawn to Anchorage because of its natural beauty and wildlife. The city is surrounded by snowcapped mountains and glaciers. The parks nearby are home to Alaskan brown bear, deer, and fur seals.

ARIZONA

Phoenix

People have been living in the Phoenix area for more than 8,000 years. The Hohokam civilization once depended on the nearby Salt River to support them. Today the river is mainly dry.

Phoenix grew to become the largest city and the capital of Arizona. Visitors to the Pueblo Grande Museum and the Heard Museum in Phoenix will find displays about the area's history.

ARKANSAS

Hot Springs

    Hot Springs is in west-central Arkansas. The city was mapped by order of Thomas Jefferson in 1804 and settled in 1807. Hot Springs is not only a city, it is a national park. The park attracts more than a million people each year. The park has more than 40 thermal, or hot, springs. Many visitors go to Bathhouse Row to bathe in the fresh hot spring water. You can also hike the trails that surround the city and camp in the beautiful park grounds.

CALIFORNIA
San Francisco

San Francisco is on the south side of the Golden Gate channel. The channel connects the Pacific Ocean with San Francisco Bay. The Famous Golden Gate Bridge spans the channel. San Francisco is also known for its cable cars that take riders up and down the city's 49 hills. Chinese culture and history are fun to explore in San Francisco's famous Chinatown.

COLORADO

Denver

Denver became the capital of the Colorado Territory in 1867. It was originally part of a small mining camp. Today Denver is the largest city in Colorado. Denver has museums of art and history including Buffalo Bill's Museum and Grave.

Nicknamed Mile High City, Denver sits about 1 mile above sea level. To the west rise the mountains of the Southern Rockies—a most impressive sight.

CONNECTICUT

Mystic

Mystic, Connecticut, is not a large town, but it has become a major tourist attraction. The area was first settled in 1654. It later became a whaling and shipbuilding center. Visitors now come to see historic ships docked along the waterfront. A re-created 19th-century village on the waterfront has become one of the area's biggest attractions.

DELAWARE
Wilmington

Wilmington is Delaware's largest city. It is located on the Delaware River. Its river location is important to the city's shipping and manufacturing industries. In fact, the Du Pont Company was established in Wilmington in 1802. It began as a producer of gunpowder. Du Pont is now one of the largest companies in the world. The Hagley Museum, the site of the first Du Pont factory, is an historic site.

FLORIDA

Miami

Miami is located in southern Florida on Biscayne Bay. It was founded in 1870. Miami began to grow into a resort area around 1900. Miami is the largest city in Florida when you include its surrounding areas, like Miami Beach to the east and Coral Gables to the south.

The Art Deco District of South Beach is a must-see. It has more than 800 buildings that look like they came right out of the Roaring '20s. The district is full of colorful shops, hotels, and people! Of course, the beaches and beautiful landscapes around the city are a must-see, too.

GEORGIA
Atlanta

Atlanta was a major Confederate supply station during the Civil War. Most of the city's buildings were burned in 1864. The Union Army's General Sherman thought that burning the city down would allow it to be built up as a better city for the future. Today Atlanta is a great new city. It has modern skyscrapers and a huge international airport. Sites and attractions in Atlanta include the CNN Center, the Margaret Mitchell (author of *Gone With the Wind*) House and Museum, and the Martin Luther King, Jr. National Historic Site.

HAWAII
Honolulu

    Honolulu, located on the island of Oahu, is Hawaii's capital and largest city. The Polynesian community on the island was discovered in 1794 by British Captain William Brown. It was in the early 1800s when the Hawaiian royal family made Honolulu their main home.

    Honolulu is a major tourist attraction. It is known for beautiful Waikiki Beach and two volcano craters, Diamond Head and the Punch Bowl. To the west is the U.S. naval base Pearl Harbor.

IDAHO
Coeur d'Alene

Located in Idaho's panhandle is the resort city of Coeur d'Alene. The city formed in 1906. It is located on the north shore of Coeur d'Alene Lake. Tourists love the scenic views from the city and visit the three National Forests nearby. Early French traders called the Native Americans there "Coeur d'Alene," meaning "sharp-hearted." The city was named for that tribe.

ILLINOIS

Chicago

Chicago lies on the southwestern shore of Lake Michigan. French explorers first set foot in the area in the late 1600s. By 1837, the area's population reached 4,000 and Chicago became a city.

This lakefront city offers something for everyone. Museums, parks, beaches, and harbors line Chicago's shoreline. You can attend professional sports games of all kinds, visit the Adler Planetarium, or learn about the Civil War and President Abraham Lincoln at the Chicago Historical Society.

INDIANA

Indianapolis

Indianapolis is the largest city in Indiana. The city is located in the middle of the state and has served as the state capital since 1825. Indianapolis is home to several great museums including one of the country's best children's museums. The area's most famous event is the

Indianapolis 500 automobile race. Other great places to visit include the Museum of Art and the Indianapolis Zoo.

IOWA

Des Moines

Fort Des Moines was built by the government in 1843 to protect the Indians in the area. In 1857 the name changed to Des Moines and the city became the capital of Iowa. Des Moines is located in the center of the country's corn-producing region. However, Des Moines is not all about

farming! The city has plenty of attractions. For instance, many people enjoy a visit to Blank Park Zoo, Living History Farms, or the historical capitol building.

KANSAS

Wichita

Wichita was settled in 1867 as a trading post. The city, named after the Wichita people, surrounds the junctions of the Arkansas and Little Arkansas Rivers. Wichita is the largest city in Kansas. Its historic landmarks include Cowtown, an area with more than two dozen buildings restored to look like the early days of Wichita. The Chisholm Trail, an 1800s cattle-driving route from Texas, passed through Wichita and helped give Cowtown its name.

KENTUCKY

Louisville

Louisville is known for its famous Kentucky Derby thoroughbred horse race, among other things. The race has been held every May since 1875. Visitors and residents of Kentucky also enjoy the Kentucky Derby Museum, the Kentucky State Fair, and the Louisville Slugger Baseball

Bat Museum. Louisville is one of the oldest settlements west of the Appalachian Mountains. It was founded in 1778.

LOUISIANA

New Orleans

New Orleans was settled by French Canadians in the early 1700s. New Orleans was once the capital of the French colony.

General Andrew Jackson defended the city from British attack in 1812 in the Battle of New Orleans. A statue of Jackson stands in Jackson Square in the French Quarter. The French Quarter is known for its Mardi Gras carnival with parades and floats.

MAINE

Augusta

    Augusta's history dates back to 1628 when it was founded by members of the Plymouth Colony of Massachusetts. In 1832 Augusta replaced Portland as the state capital.

    Fort Western is the oldest surviving structure in the area. The fort has been restored and is now a museum. The Maine State Museum is also in Augusta. Tourism and government services are important to the city's economy.

MARYLAND

Baltimore

Baltimore is a port city on Chesapeake Bay and is the largest city in Maryland. It was explored by John Smith in 1608, but not settled by the English until 1661.

Baltimore has many historical sites to visit. Some include the city zoo and conservatory, Fort McHenry National Monument and Historic Shrine, and Babe Ruth's birthplace. The city also has monuments to Christopher Columbus and George Washington.

MASSACHUSETTS
Boston

Boston's many historical sites are connected by the Freedom Trail. It is a self-guided walking tour that includes Paul Revere's House and the Old State House. The Black Heritage Trail includes the Hayden House, which was part of the Underground Railroad.

Many important events of the American Revolution occurred in the Boston area; for example, the Boston Tea Party of 1773, the Battles of Lexington and Concord, and the Battle of Bunker Hill in 1775.

MICHIGAN
Detroit

Detroit is Michigan's largest city. The Wyandot people lived in the Detroit area before the first Europeans arrived. History buffs can visit the Great Lakes Indian Museum and the Fort Wayne Military Museum.

Detroit is home to major league baseball, football, hockey, and basketball. It is also known as Motor City because it makes the largest percentage of the nation's automobiles.

MINNESOTA

Minneapolis

Minneapolis is a Sioux Indian name meaning "water." The city is surrounded by many lakes and rivers. The Mississippi and Minnesota Rivers come together at Minneapolis. Saint Anthony Falls in downtown Minneapolis is a 65 foot (20 m) drop in the Mississippi River. Historic Fort Snelling was built in 1819 to help settlers move west. Today Minneapolis is the largest city in the state and shares the title "Twin Cities" with St. Paul, the state capital.

MISSISSIPPI

Vicksburg

Vicksburg is a major port on the Mississippi River. The city is named after its founder Newitt Vick, a Methodist minister who settled there in 1812. Vicksburg was the site of a major battle during the Civil War. Union troops commanded by General Grant captured the city from the Confederates. Nearby Vicksburg National Military Park contains monuments and memorials to the 47-day battle.

MISSOURI

St. Louis

St. Louis was settled by French fur trader Pierre Laclède in 1764. The city has grown from a small trading post to a major transportation and manufacturing center.

St. Louis attractions and sites include Laclède's Landing, a historical riverfront area, and the Gateway Arch, representing St. Louis as the gateway to the West. West of downtown is Forest Park, which has the St. Louis Zoo, the History Museum, the Art Museum, and the Science Center.

MONTANA

Helena

    Helena is the capital of Montana. It is surrounded by beautiful hills, rocky mountains, forests, and parks.

    The Helena area was explored by the Lewis and Clark expedition in 1805. It became a supply center for area mining camps. The area grew when gold was discovered there in 1864. Last Chance Gulch, Helena's name back then, is now an historical site on Main Street.

NEBRASKA

Omaha

Omaha was named for the Omaha Native American tribe that lived in the area. The city's location near the center of the U.S. made it an important trading and transportation center. In the 1800s, wagon trains heading west often began their journey there. Omaha is the largest city in Nebraska. Favorite local attractions include museums and a zoo for rare species.

NEVADA

Las Vegas

Gambling casinos are illegal in most U.S. cities, but they are what Las Vegas is famous for. Flashy neon signs and fancy hotels and casinos welcome millions of visitors to the city every year. Gambling is not the only attraction in Las Vegas. Famous comedians, singers, dancers, and other personalities perform there regularly. Other local attractions include museums, Hoover Dam, and the Lake Mead National Recreation Area.

NEW HAMPSHIRE

Concord

Concord is a small city located on the Merrimack River in southern New Hampshire. Concord has been the capital of New Hampshire since 1808. The city is famous for Concord granite that is found nearby. The Library of Congress in Washington D.C. was built with the beautiful white granite. Tourists to the area enjoy visiting the home of President Franklin Pierce and the State Historical Society Museum.

NEW JERSEY

Atlantic City

Atlantic City is a resort town on a small island in New Jersey. It is a popular place for conventions because of its large convention center and its fun attractions. Atlantic City has a famous 6-mile (9.65 km) long boardwalk that includes amusement parks, restaurants, and shops. The city is also home to several big gambling casinos.

NEW MEXICO

Santa Fe

The Spanish founded Santa Fe in 1610 to serve as the capital of New Mexico. Control of the area was taken by Mexico in 1821. After the Mexican War in 1848, New Mexico became a part of the United.States. Santa Fe's rich history can be seen in its many museums and historical buildings. Santa Fe's location near the Sangre de Cristo Mountains makes it a year-round tourist center.

NEW YORK

New York City

Millions of people call New York City home. In fact, the city is the largest in the United States. New York City is actually divided into five areas called boroughs. Four of the five boroughs are located on islands. The area's first inhabitants were Algonquian and Iroquois Native Americans. The population now includes people from all over the world. New York City is home to great museums, professional sports teams, symphonies, orchestras, and theaters. New York City is also famous for its tall skyscrapers.

North Carolina

Charlotte

Charlotte is the largest city in North Carolina. The city was named after the wife of King George III of Great Britain. Charlotte has become an important financial center. It is home to the Carolina Panthers pro football team and the Charlotte Hornets pro basketball team. Charlotte's location between the mountains and the ocean makes it a popular place to live and visit.

North Dakota

Bismarck

The site of present-day Bismarck was once used by Native Americans as a place to cross the Missouri River. The area is now the capital and one of the largest cities in North Dakota. Discovery of gold in the nearby Black Hills in 1874 helped the city grow quickly. One popular tourist attraction is Fort Lincoln. The fort was once commanded by Lieutenant Colonel George Custer, who was later killed at the Battle of Little Bighorn. The site is now a state park.

OHIO

Cincinnati

Cincinnati sits on the banks of the Ohio River in southwest Ohio. The area was first inhabited by Native Americans. The first white settlement was Losantiville, built in 1788. Losantiville was renamed Cincinnati in 1790. Cincinnati was an important stop on the Underground Railroad that helped slaves escape from the South. Today visitors enjoy professional baseball, football, a world-class symphony orchestra, and one of the world's best zoos.

OKLAHOMA

Oklahoma City

Oklahoma City had an interesting start. On April 22, 1889, a tent city of more than 10,000 people sprang up overnight after President Hayes opened the area to settlement.

Modern-day Oklahoma City is a fun place to visit. Unusual sites like the National Cowboy Hall of Fame, the National Softball Hall of Fame, and the Photography Hall of Fame give the city character. More common attractions like the Oklahoma City Zoo and the Museum of Art are popular, too.

OREGON

Portland

The first residents of Portland, Oregon, named their new settlement after their hometown, Portland, Maine. During the California gold rush, travelers stopped there to get supplies. This helped the city to grow quickly. The city grew even faster after a railroad was completed connecting Portland to the eastern U.S. The city is now home to several fine colleges, a ballet theater, and a zoo. Portland is a popular tourist area because of its location between the Pacific Ocean and nearby mountains.

PENNSYLVANIA

Philadelphia

Philadelphia is one of the most historical places in the U.S. Both the Declaration of Independence and the U.S. Constitution were written there. One of the nation's oldest cities, Philadelphia is also the fifth largest. People are attracted to the area's historical landmarks. Great places to visit include Independence Hall, the Liberty Bell, and the Betsy Ross House.

RHODE ISLAND

Newport

 Newport has long been a favorite vacation spot for sailors and fishermen. The Americas Cup sailboat race was held there from 1930-1983. The city was founded in 1639 as a "new port." It quickly grew into a major trading and shipbuilding center. Newport attractions include the International Tennis Hall of Fame and Museum and The Breakers, a famous mansion.

SOUTH CAROLINA
Charleston

Charleston was founded more than 300 years ago in 1670. It was first named Charles Town in honor of the King of England. The ocean harbor at Charleston is home to one of the busiest ports in the southeastern U.S. Charleston has many historic places to visit. Interesting sites include old forts such as Fort Sumter, where the first battle of the Civil War occurred. Another great place to visit is Charleston's historic district.

SOUTH DAKOTA
Rapid City

Rapid City is in southwestern South Dakota. It is located on Rapid Creek at the base of the Black Hills. Rapid City is a mining, ranching, and grain-producing city. However, tourism is important to the area. Families enjoy the Museum of Geology and Dinosaur Park. Rapid City also acts as the entrance to the Black Hills. Black Hills attractions include Mount Rushmore and Custer State Park.

TENNESSEE

Nashville

Nashville has many fine attractions, but it is famous for its country and western music. Nashville has been a center for country and western music performers since the 1920's. Performers go there not only to perform, but also to record their music. One of Nashville's most popular attractions is the Grand Ole Opry.

Texas

Houston

The first settlement in this area was built in 1826. Named after a military general, Houston became a city in 1839. The city began to grow after the discovery of oil and natural gas in nearby salt domes. One of the city's most famous sites is the Lyndon B. Johnson Space Center. The center controls all U.S. manned space flights.

UTAH

Salt Lake City

The Mormons settled Salt Lake City in 1847. Since then, Salt Lake City has become the largest city in Utah. The city is named after nearby Great Salt Lake. The area is well known for its world-class skiing and winter sports. Because of its attractions, Salt Lake City was chosen as the home of the 2002 Winter Olympics.

VERMONT
Burlington

Burlington, Vermont's largest city, is located on Lake Champlain's eastern shore. Like many of the smaller cities in Vermont, Burlington is a tourist area. The Green Mountains just east of Burlington have many camping areas, ski resorts, and, of course, show off beautiful color in the fall. The city itself is home to Ethan Allen Farm. Revolutionary War hero Ethan Allen lived in Burlington and is buried there.

VIRGINIA

Richmond

Richmond is the modern-day capital of Virginia. It first became a city in 1782, but its history goes back much farther. The area was visited by Captain John Smith in 1607. Settlers soon followed and built a settlement in 1637. During the Civil War, Richmond served as the capital of the Confederacy. Visitors should see the State Capitol designed by Thomas Jefferson and the Edgar Allan Poe museum.

WASHINGTON

Seattle

Seattle was named for Chief Seattle of the Suquamish Native American tribe. The Suquamish lived in this area before the city was founded. Today Seattle is the most populated city in Washington. It is surrounded by mountains including Mount Rainier, a dormant volcano. Seattle is home to professional sports teams, a symphony orchestra, and many popular museums. One of Seattle's most famous sites is the Space Needle, which stands over 607 feet (185 m) tall.

WEST VIRGINIA

Charleston

Charleston is the largest city in West Virginia and its capital. It is located where the Elk and Kanahwa Rivers merge. Charleston started as a frontier post in 1788. Frontiersman Daniel Boone made Charleston a major stop during his travels into the Ohio Valley. The city's Coonskin Park is named for its frontier history. Other points of interest include the State Capitol, completed in 1932, and the Sunrise Mansion.

WISCONSIN

Milwaukee

The Potawatomi Native Americans called this place *Mahn-ah-wauk*. The name means "gathering place by the water." It's easy to see why the Potawatomi used this name. The city is located on Lake Michigan near the junction of three rivers. Milwaukee is a major port for ships using the Great Lakes-Saint Lawrence Seaway system. Tourists can visit the Milwaukee Zoo or attend a professional baseball or basketball game.

WYOMING

Jackson

Most people who visit Wyoming come to see the famous natural beauty of the area. Jackson's location near many of the state's attractions helped it become a major tourist stop. Wild rivers, canyons, mountains, and large areas of wilderness surround Jackson. The Jackson area is also famous for its wildlife including bear, moose, and elk. Wyoming's most popular ski resorts are also nearby. Jackson was named after American fur trapper David Jackson.